Blueberry Hill
The Power of Love

By: Deborah Lynn Darling

Illustrated By: Robert Jursinski

Radiance Publishing

Radiance Publishing
P.O. Box 98
Garrettsville, Ohio 44231

**Blueberry Hill
The Power of Love**

Library of Congress Catalogue Card Number 98-92129
ISBN: 0-9667111-0-6
First edition 1998   10 9 8 7 6 5 4 3 2 1

This book is dedicated to Blueberry Hill for bringing such joy into my life and to the people of Garrettsville who have welcomed me and made me feel at home.

Once upon a time,
in a town called Garrettsville,
An old and weathered lifeless house
was sitting on a hill

People would drive by the house,
barely noticing it was there
For the house had been neglected and
was in great need of care

The house had not felt love nor care
in oh, so many years
The truth be known,
the old weathered house sat
day in and out in tears

Yearning for a magic time,
within the not too distant future
When it would once again
be lived in, loved and nurtured

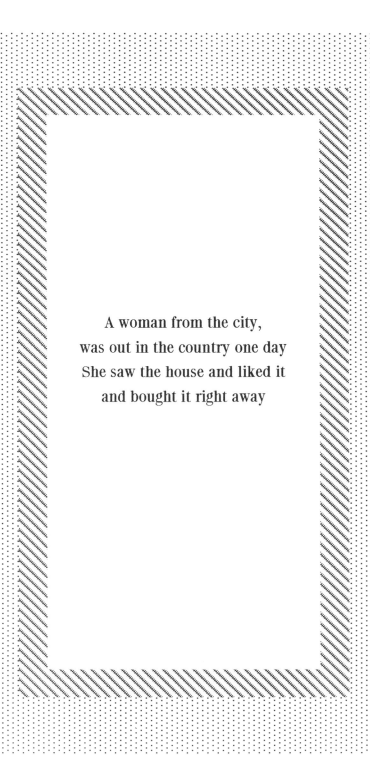

A woman from the city,
was out in the country one day
She saw the house and liked it
and bought it right away

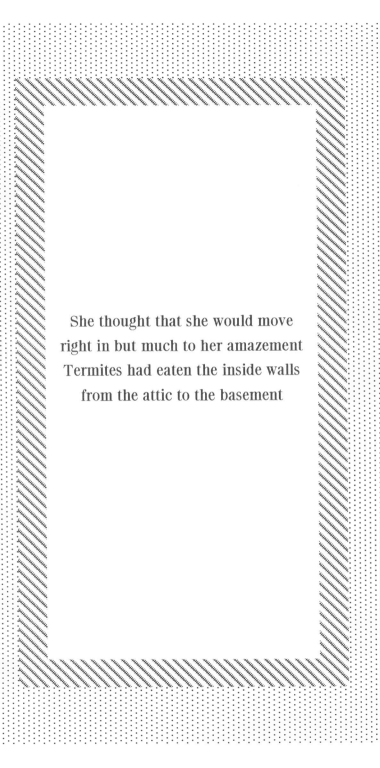

She thought that she would move
right in but much to her amazement
Termites had eaten the inside walls
from the attic to the basement

She loved the old and weathered
house so dearly even then
That she hired an entire crew to
build it back again

They worked on the house
for one whole year
and after they were through
The woman from the city
had plenty left to do

She decorated every room
with lots of love and care
She no longer had to search for "home"
cause she was living there

The house and she were bonded,
of that there could be no denial
She loved the house and it appeared
that the house was beginning to smile

The woman too had not felt love in
such a long, long time
The house was helping her to heal
the wounds she'd left behind

While growing up she lived in many
houses, apartments and such
But never did she call them home,
until this house she loved so much

She painted her new love,
two gorgeous shades of blue
With little yellow accents
until it looked brand new

The house now looked quite stately,
not one bit run of the mill
Since it sat on a hill and was
blueberry colored,
she named it Blueberry Hill

With every day at Blueberry Hill, she
grew more and more peaceful inside
The house was healing all the pain
she no longer needed to hide

The woman loved the house so much
that she wanted others to share
In the loving, nurturing environment
that she'd created there

She opened the house as a B&B,
where those visiting town could stay
The list of guests just grew and grew
with every passing day

People so loved the charming house
and all it had to show
That they were often saddened
when it was time to go

They hated to leave this peaceful
place and venture on their way
And they would always mention
they'd be back again someday

One day a lovely visitor
arrived at Blueberry Hill
She seemed so sad and empty
and said she was feeling ill

She said her head was spinning
with hundreds of thoughts in her mind
And she had to find a quiet place
where she could just unwind

She said she'd heard of Blueberry Hill
while reading the Sunday news
And she needed time to relax
and think, to clear away her blues

She walked around the grounds awhile
and went to bed early that night
When she came downstairs the next
morning, she looked happy, cheerful
and bright

She said she awoke at 3:00 a.m.
and at the foot of her bed
Stood an older blond haired woman,
with her hair pulled back on her head

She was not afraid of the woman,
who had soft and gentle eyes
But said the woman's presence there
was rather a surprise

The woman never said a word
as she smiled at the girl in bed
But all at once the unceasing thoughts
just vanished from her head

She fell back to sleep more soundly
than she had slept before
And when she awoke she realized
her troubles were no more

The woman had somehow transferred
thoughts, without a single word
And the visitor knew what had to be
done, from the message she had heard

The woman told her
that things would be fine,
there was no need to worry and longer
The visitor knew that in a short time
she'd feel happier, healthier
and stronger

The visitor relayed this message,
when she came downstairs to dine
She said she felt much better
and would be back another time

She'd often visit Blueberry Hill
when she was feeling blue
And the older woman
with the blond pulled back hair,
would tell her what to do

Others came to visit
and reported the woman as well
They all had pleasant experiences
and were very eager to tell

It was as if they'd seen an angel
for they spoke of lovely things
Of inner peace and harmony
and the joy that love can bring

It seemed the house was magical,
wild animals came to explore
The inside animals and outside
animals would sit face to face
at the door

Maddie, the cocker spaniel
and Maxwell the terrier too
Would play outside on the rolling hills,
there was just so much to do

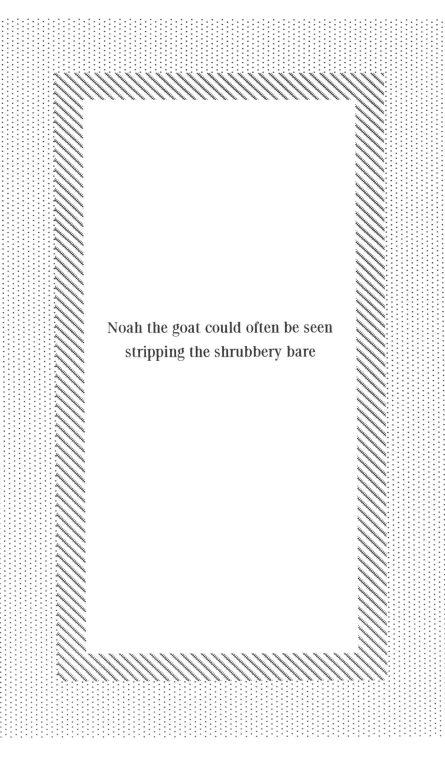

Noah the goat could often be seen
stripping the shrubbery bare

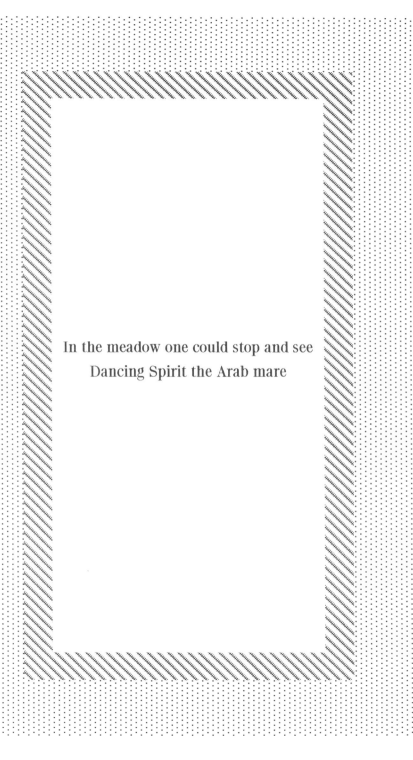

In the meadow one could stop and see
Dancing Spirit the Arab mare

Dalai, the indoor kitty
exemplified pure joy
She loved everyone without judgement
be they young or old, girl or boy

Loki, the wild outdoor kitty,
the neighbors would always bet
Might be given a name
but would never be tamed
they were stunned he became a pet

When the woman would venture
out into the yard,
during the course of the day
Both the tame and wild animals
would come around and play

The woman so loved nature
and all its little creatures
That she listed them on her brochure
as part of the special features

The animals were not afraid
of this woman one little bit
And she was not afraid of them
no fear did she emit

They all communed together
at this blue house on the hill
The tame and wild animals
would sit so close and still

The woman spoke kind words to them
and told them how lovely they were
And they would return day after day
just to get some love from her

The woman could not speak to them
in their native tongues
But she spoke to them in the language,
of the *Universal One*

The language we all know as "love"
is powerful no doubt
It's the only language on the earth
that everything figures out

For love is all it really takes
to mend what's been torn apart
To fix the broken fences
in the recesses of one's heart

Blueberry Hill appears peaceful now
to those who daily pass by
Perhaps the woman's love for the house
is the major reason why

For a woman from the city
shared her love with this house on a hill
And the house feels loved and cared for
by the woman who lives there still

The woman's quite contented now
she has no more need to roam
For the house she's loved and cared for
has given her a home

When you find someone or something
that's quite precious and dear to you
Love it and treat it kindly
that's all you need to do

When you watch
that which you cherish
grow from the seed of your love
You know that something wonderful's
been designed by God above

For that which one tends with their
heart, reaps the benefits one sows
It's the Universal language of love
a language each <u>already</u> knows

The magic of love from Blueberry Hill
is within your heart so clear
Express your joy and share your love
with all who venture near

You don't need to visit Blueberry Hill
to know what love's all about
If you look around
at your family and friends
I am sure you will figure it out

Make a list of all the people and
things that you love:

1._____
2._____
3._____
4._____
5._____
6._____
7._____
8._____
9._____
10._____
11._____
12._____
13._____
14._____
15._____
16._____
17._____
18._____
19._____
20._____

Make a list of all the people and
things you are grateful for:

1._____

2._____

3._____

4._____

5._____

6._____

7._____

8._____

9._____

10._____

11._____

12._____

13._____

14._____

15._____

16._____

17._____

18._____

19._____

20._____

Make a list of the qualities you love about yourself:

1._____
2._____
3._____
4._____
5._____
6._____
7._____
8._____
9._____
10._____
11._____
12._____
13._____
14._____
15._____
16._____
17._____
18._____
19._____
20._____

Make a list of the qualities you look for in a friend:

1._____
2._____
3._____
4._____
5._____
6._____
7._____
8._____
9._____
10._____
11._____
12._____
13._____
14._____
15._____
16._____
17._____
18._____
19._____
20._____

Make a list of all the things you could do today to become a better person:

1._____
2._____
3._____
4._____
5._____
6._____
7._____
8._____
9._____
10._____
11._____
12._____
13._____
14._____
15._____
16._____
17._____
18._____
19._____
20._____

Make a list of all the people you need
to forgive:

1._____
2._____
3._____
4._____
5._____
6._____
7._____
8._____
9._____
10._____
11._____
12._____
13._____
14._____
15._____
16._____
17._____
18._____
19._____
20._____

Make a list of all the people who need to forgive you:

1. _____
2. _____
3. _____
4. _____
5. _____
6. _____
7. _____
8. _____
9. _____
10. _____
11. _____
12. _____
13. _____
14. _____
15. _____
16. _____
17. _____
18. _____
19. _____
20. _____

Make a list of all the things you
would like to accomplish.

1._____
2._____
3._____
4._____
5._____
6._____
7._____
8._____
9._____
10._____
11._____
12._____
13._____
14._____
15._____
16._____
17._____
18._____
19._____
20._____

You can order additional copies of
Blueberry Hill The Power of Love
by calling Radiance Publishing at (330) 527-2407
or by writing:

Radiance Publishing
P.O. Box 98
Garrettsville, Ohio 44231